THE THREE PRINCES

I see your invisible
crown and will
always love you.
xoxo !
Grandy

THE EXCHANGE

**Is it better
to work together
or alone?
When?**

THE THREE PRINCES

A Tale from the Middle East

retold by Eric A. Kimmel

illustrated by Leonard Everett Fisher

HAMPTON-BROWN

Notes About the Book

The story of "The Three Princes" is known throughout the Middle East. I first heard it in 1983, when I was teaching a class in storytelling at Portland State University. Several of my students were from Saudi Arabia. "The Three Princes" was one of many wonderful stories they shared with me. Since then, I have come across Egyptian, Moroccan, and Persian versions of the tale. It also appears in later editions of the collection of stories known as *The Arabian Nights*.

—E.A.K.

During World War II, I served with the U.S. Army Corps of Engineers in Morocco and Algeria. I became intrigued with the Muslim culture I found there. Illustrating "The Three Princes" provided me with an opportunity to recreate the essence of the Arab world.

I prepared the art by painting illustration boards black, then drawing my designs on them with white chalk. The chalk drawings and black under-painting disappeared beneath a final application of acrylic color.

—L.E.F.

To Doris Kimmel—wise as well as beautiful

E.A.K.

To Margery Fisher—beautiful as well as wise

L.E.F.

The Three Princes retold by Eric A. Kimmel, illustrated by Leonard Everett Fisher. Text copyright © 1994 by Eric A. Kimmel. Illustrations copyright © 1994 by Leonard Everett Fisher. All rights reserved. Reprinted by permission of Holiday House, Inc.

Introductions, questions, on-page glossaries, The Exchange © Hampton-Brown.

Hampton-Brown
P.O. Box 223220
Carmel, California 93922
800-333-3510
www.hampton-brown.com

Printed in the United States of America

ISBN: 0-7362-2776-8

05 06 07 08 09 10 11 12 13 14 10 9 8 7 6 5 4 3 2 1

The princess decides she will marry the man who brings her the best gift. One prince finds a crystal ball, one finds a magic carpet, and Prince Mohsen finds a special orange.

Once there was and once there was not a princess who was **as wise as she was** beautiful. Princes from all over the world **sought her hand in marriage**, but the ones she liked best were three cousins: Prince Fahad, Prince Muhammed, and Prince Mohsen.

Once there was and once there was not This is a story about

as wise as she was wise and

sought her hand in marriage wanted to marry her

Prince Fahad and Prince Muhammed were **men of wealth and renown**, although they were neither young nor handsome. Prince Mohsen, by contrast, was tall and slender as a **reed**. His flashing eyes **melted the princess's heart** the first time she saw him. However, as the youngest son of a poor king, Prince Mohsen **possessed little more than** his handsome face, his cloak, and his camel. Nonetheless, he was the one the princess loved and the one she was determined to marry.

men of wealth and renown rich and famous men
reed long, thin plant
melted the princess's heart made the princess love him
possessed little more than had only

The wazir, her chief minister, **scoffed** at her decision. "Mohsen? He has nothing to give you."

"Then I will give him a chance to find something," the princess said. **Summoning** the three princes, she said to them, "Go out into the world for a year and bring back the **rarest thing you find in your travels.** I will marry the prince who returns with the **greatest wonder.**"

scoffed laughed

Summoning Calling

rarest thing you find in your travels most wonderful thing you can find

greatest wonder best gift

The next morning the three princes **rode out** together. They traveled across the desert for many days until they came to a place where the path **branched off** in three directions.

"This is a sign that we should separate," Prince Fahad said.

Prince Muhammed and Prince Mohsen agreed. Prince Fahad took the path to the right, Prince Muhammed took the path to the left, and Prince Mohsen continued straight on across the desert.

rode out left
branched off split, separated

BEFORE YOU MOVE ON...

1. **Comparisons** Reread page 7. How are the princes alike and different?

2. **Conclusions** Reread page 9. The princess sent the three princes to bring her the rarest thing. How could this help her marry Prince Mohsen?

LOOK AHEAD Are the princes' gifts wonderful enough? Read pages 12–17 to find out.

After **one year's time** they returned to the place where the three paths met. They camped for the night, sharing stories of their adventures. One by one the stars came out.

"What great wonder did you find on your travels?" Prince Fahad asked Prince Muhammed.

Prince Muhammed replied, "I traveled across the Iron Mountains to the **distant** Hadramaut. In a cave guarded by a **frightful djinn**, I found a great wonder." He reached under his cloak and took out a crystal ball.

"A crystal ball? What is so wonderful about that?" his cousins asked.

"This is no **ordinary** crystal ball," Prince Muhammed replied. "When I **peer** inside it, I can see what is happening anywhere in the world. Is that not a wonderful thing?"

His cousins agreed that it was.

one year's time a year
distant far away place called
frightful djinn scary spirit
ordinary normal
peer look

Prince Muhammed turned to Prince Fahad. "What wonder did you bring back from your travels?"

Prince Fahad answered, "I traveled across Egypt's desert sands. In the **tomb of a forgotten king**, I discovered this." He unwrapped a bundle and spread it on the ground. It was a carpet.

"A carpet? What is so wonderful about that?" Prince Muhammed and Prince Mohsen asked him.

Prince Fahad replied, "This is a flying carpet. It can carry me wherever I want to go in less time than it takes to tell about it. Is that not a wonderful thing?"

His cousins agreed that it was.

tomb of a forgotten king grave of a king who people forgot

Then Prince Fahad and Prince Muhammed turned to Prince Mohsen. "What rare and wonderful thing did you find on your travels?" they asked.

"I journeyed to the shores of the Great Sea," Prince Mohsen replied. "There I met a sailor who gave me this!" He opened his hand and held out an orange.

His cousins began to laugh. "Is that all? An ordinary orange?"

"This is not an ordinary orange!" Prince Mohsen protested. "It is **a healing orange**. It can cure any illness, even if a person is dying."

"If what you say is true, then this orange is the greatest wonder of all," the other two princes said. However, they did not sound as if they really believed it.

a healing orange an orange that can stop sickness and death

BEFORE YOU MOVE ON...

1. **Summarize** All of the gifts seemed ordinary at first. What was wonderful about each gift?

2. **Conclusions** The princess said the gifts must be rare. What shows that they are?

LOOK AHEAD Read pages 18–25 to find how valuable each gift really is.

As the three princes sat under the **starry sky**, Prince Mohsen happened to **remark**, "I wonder if the princess is well. We have not seen her in a year."

"Gather around," Prince Muhammed said. "My crystal ball can show her to us." The three princes peered inside the crystal ball together.

starry sky sky full of stars
remark say

19

A tragic scene appeared before their eyes. There lay the princess, **pale as death**. The wazir and the ladies and gentlemen of her court stood around her bed, weeping. Doctors bent over her, shaking their heads. The princes lowered their ears to the crystal ball and found they could hear what the doctors were saying. "Our princess is dying. She will not live to see the sun rise."

"The princess needn't die. My orange can cure her," Prince Mohsen cried. "But how can I reach her in time? Even if I rode all night, I could never arrive by morning."

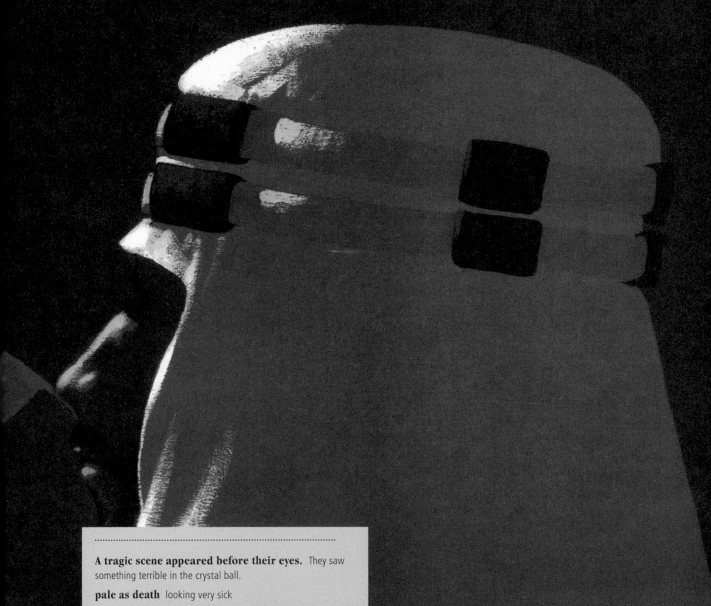

....

A tragic scene appeared before their eyes. They saw something terrible in the crystal ball.

pale as death looking very sick

"My carpet can carry us there **in an instant**," Prince Fahad said. "Quick, get on!"

The three princes leaped onto the flying carpet. In less time than it takes to tell about it, the carpet **whisked** them through the air all the way to the princess's palace. The princes ran through the gates, crying, "Clear the way! Let us through!" **Crowds of courtiers parted** to let them pass.

in an instant very quickly

whisked carried

Crowds of courtiers parted Many people who lived in the palace moved

23

Prince Mohsen knelt beside the dying princess. He cut the healing orange into four pieces. As soon as the princess tasted the first piece, **her color returned**. The second piece, and her eyes opened. The third, and she sat up in bed. By the time she finished the last piece, she was **completely cured**.

"**A miracle!**" the wazir cried. The courtiers echoed, "A miracle!"

"It is a miracle indeed," the princess said. "These three noble princes have restored me to life. I will marry the prince who was most responsible for saving me."

---

her color returned she began to look healthier
completely cured no longer sick
A miracle! It's amazing!

BEFORE YOU MOVE ON...

1. **Cause and Effect** How did each gift help save the princess?

2. **Context Clues** Reread page 25. What clues tell you that "restored me to life" means "stopped me from dying"?

LOOK AHEAD Read pages 26–32 to find out how the princess decides which gift is best.

"Which one is that?" everyone asked.

"The princess obviously means Prince Mohsen, for it was his orange that cured her," the doctors said.

"True," the courtiers replied. "But the orange had to arrive in time to be **of any use**. Prince Fahad's magic carpet brought it here, so he is the one who really saved her."

"But neither the orange nor the carpet would have **done any good** if the princes had not known that the princess was dying," the wazir pointed out. "I say it was Prince Muhammed's crystal ball that was most responsible for restoring our princess to life."

of any use helpful
done any good saved her

The doctors and the courtiers and the wazir argued and argued, but could not agree. So in the end they did what they should have done in the beginning. They asked the princess.

"Which prince truly saved your life? Which one are you going to marry?"

The princess answered, "No prince could have saved me by himself. Each needed the help of his companions. **All three played an equal part**, and I **am grateful to** them all."

"But you cannot marry them all!" the wazir protested.

"I know. I must choose one . . . and the one I choose is—Prince Mohsen!"

"Mohsen? Why not Muhammed? Why not Fahad?" everyone asked.

All three played an equal part Every prince helped
am grateful to want to thank

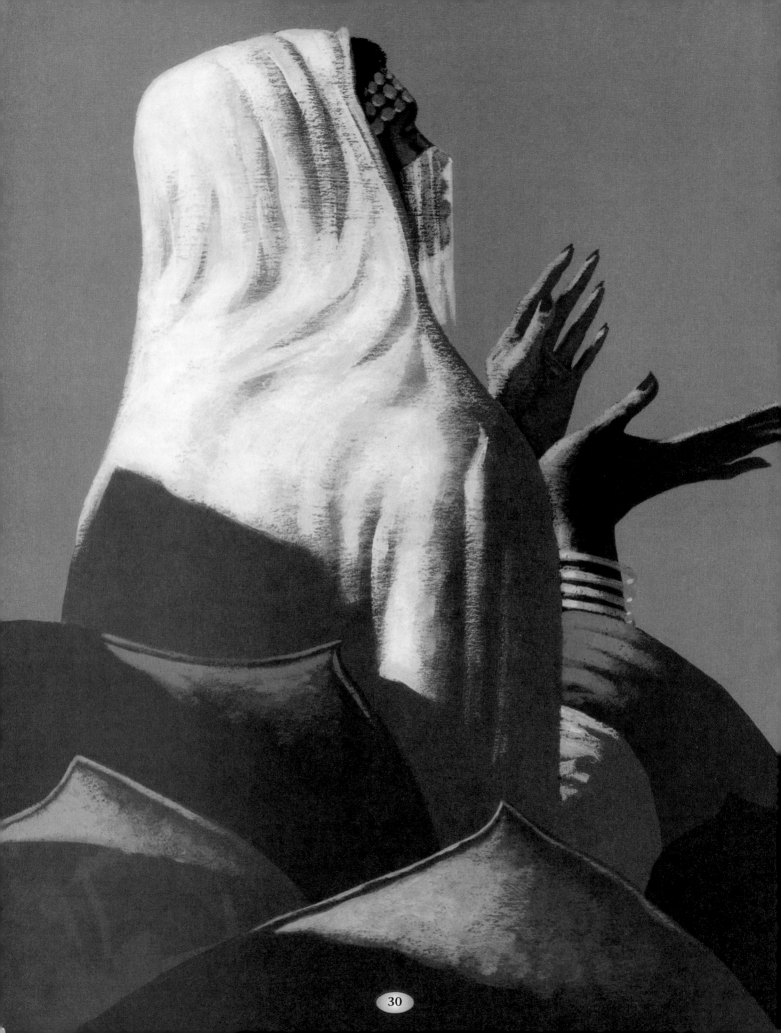

The princess summoned the three princes to kneel before her.

"Prince Fahad," she said, "do you still have your flying carpet?"

"I do."

"Prince Muhammed, do you still have your crystal ball?"

"I do."

"And **what of you**, Mohsen? Where is your magic orange?"

"I **gave it up** to save your life, Princess," he answered.

"You see how it is," the princess told her courtiers. "Prince Muhammed and Prince Fahad have lost nothing. Each still has his crystal ball and flying carpet. With these wonders added to the wealth and renown they already possess, they will have no trouble finding other princesses to marry. But Prince Mohsen gave up his orange, his only possession, to save me. He was the one who **sacrificed** the most. I cannot restore his orange. However, I can give him something of equal value. I can become his bride."

what of you what about you
gave it up let you eat it
sacrificed gave

Thus it was said, and thus it was done. Prince Fahad and Prince Muhammed found other princesses to marry, equally beautiful, if not as wise. And the princess who was as wise as she was beautiful—which made her more beautiful still—and Prince Mohsen, who had **won her heart from the first**, lived together in joy and delight **to the end of their days**.

Thus it was said, and thus it was done. So this is how the story ends.

won her heart from the first made her love him the first time they saw each other

to the end of their days forever

BEFORE YOU MOVE ON...

1. **Conclusions** The princess decided that the orange was the best gift. Why was it difficult to decide?

2. **Plot** Reread page 31. Why did the princess ask each prince if he still had his gift?

Review the work you did in your Journal. Take your book and your Journal with you to The Exchange book discussion.

EXCHANGE IDEAS

Q **What do you think about this book?**
- What did you like best? What did you like least?
- What other stories have you read like this?
- Would you tell a friend to read this book? Why or why not?

Q **How was the problem solved?**
- Use your Problem and Solution Chart as you share ideas.

Q **And what about that big question?**

> **Is it better to work together or alone? When?**

- How would the three princes answer this question?

- The three princes have to work together. Have you ever had to work in a group to solve a problem? What did you like about it? What did you not like?

- What if only two of the princes agreed to work together and the third did not? Tell about a time when working in a group was difficult.

REFLECT

Write about your Exchange. Tell if you changed your mind about something, or saw something in a different way.

Many men want to marry the beautiful
and wise princess. So she decides to give
three of them a test. She will marry the
prince who brings her the best gift. Each
prince finds something wonderful—a
crystal ball, a magic carpet, and an orange
that can heal sickness. But while the
three princes are searching the world, the
princess gets sick. Only when the princes
use the gifts together can they save the
princess. Now the question is—whose gift
was the best? Who will marry the princess?

HAMPTON-BROWN
800-333-3510
www.hampton-brown.com

Plymouth Colony and Squanto

The **Pilgrims** were English colonists who founded Plymouth Colony in present-day Massachusetts, in December of 1620. By the spring of 1621, almost half of the people in Plymouth Colony had died of sickness and starvation. In March of 1621, a Native man named Tisquantum (Squanto) arrived at the colony. He had been to England and knew how to speak English, so he acted as a translator between the Pilgrims and the leaders of the nations in the area. The Pilgrims and the Native nations had been fighting, but Squanto helped establish a peace agreement between them. To encourage peace, Squanto shared his knowledge with the Pilgrims. Squanto taught the Pilgrims how to grow and harvest crops and how to fish and hunt. He showed them the best places to gather foods and taught them which plants were poisonous and which were useful. Without Squanto's help, the Pilgrims may not have survived for long.

The fur trade

During the 1600s, Native nations also played key roles in the **fur trade** and in France and England's fight to control it. Native trappers provided all the furs that were shipped to Europe, where they were made into fashionable hats and clothing. Various Native nations formed **alliances** with either the French or the English. England's alliances with Native nations helped them defeat the French and take control of North America in 1763. The fur trade remained an important part of North America's **economy** until the 1800s. The countries of Canada and the United States exist as they do today in part because of the actions of Native people hundreds of years ago.

Foods and cooking

Many of the foods found in grocery stores and markets today were first grown by Native North Americans. In fact, almost half of all the food in the world comes from plants that Native people **domesticated**. To domesticate means to change wild plants so that they are more useful to people.

Native North Americans domesticated at least 40 different kinds of wild plants for use as foods and medicines. Native farmers raised corn, beans, sweet potatoes, squash, pine nuts, and sunflower seeds for food. Today, these crops feed hundreds of millions of people around the world!

Corn

Today, corn is an important crop in all parts of the world because it is easy to grow and because each harvest produces a lot of food. Hundreds of years ago, corn was the main crop grown in North America. The people of each nation developed **varieties**, or types, of corn that grew best in the soil and weather conditions in the nation's territory. Over time, Native people developed hundreds of varieties of corn.

Food for the world

Soon after the colonists learned how to grow and use corn, they sent corn plants to Europe. People around the world realized that corn could feed many people. Some historians believe that the world's **population**, or the number of people in the world, grew a lot between the 1600s and 1800s because corn saved people from starving. Today, corn has more than 3,500 uses. It is used to make laundry detergent, **biodegradable** plastic, ink, diapers, and fuels.

Did you know?

Native foods and recipes are part of many people's diets, although most people do not realize it. Some of the most popular "Canadian" and "American" foods, such as turkey, maple syrup, corn on the cob, pumpkins, squash, and cranberries, come from traditional Native North American recipes. People from the Wampanoag nation shared several of these foods at a feast with the Pilgrims in 1621. Many people refer to this feast the "first" Thanksgiving, but Native nations across North America have held feasts and celebrations to offer thanks for harvests for thousands of years.

Famous foods

There are many well-known foods and flavors that are based on Native American recipes. How many of these foods do you recognize? Did you know that they began as Native American foods?

- baked beans
- baked clams
- corn chowder—a thick soup made with corn, potatoes, and onions
- corn pone—flat corn bread or cakes originally cooked in hot ashes
- filé gumbo—a type of stew thickened with sassafras
- grits—a dish of coarsely ground corn kernels made with water or milk
- hominy—coarsely ground corn used to make grits
- hush puppies—deep-fried cornmeal dough
- jerky—long, thin strips of dried meat
- popcorn
- roasted corn on the cob
- roast turkey
- succotash—a dish of corn and lima beans cooked together
- trail mix—a mixture of seeds, nuts, and dried berries

Wild foods

Native people gathered many wild foods, including wild rice, berries such as blueberries, strawberries, and cranberries, and nuts such as acorns, walnuts, pecans, and hickory nuts. They shared these foods with the colonists. The foods have since become popular all around the world. Although Native people did not raise these plants, they **cultivated** them, or helped them grow.

Transportation

Native North Americans moved from place to place to hunt, fish, gather foods, and trade with people from other nations. They made a variety of boats, snowshoes, and toboggans for use in travel. The oceans and the many rivers, lakes, and streams were some of the fastest and easiest travel routes. To travel across the land, Native nations marked numerous paths and trails through forests, over mountains, and across grasslands.

Canoes

Many Native groups used boats to transport themselves and their goods from place to place. Most built canoes, which they used for hunting, fishing, gathering food, for traveling to trade, and for moving from place to place as the seasons changed. The canoes were lightweight but very sturdy. They could be paddled and steered easily in streams and rivers, and they were light enough to **portage**, or carry over land. Canoes were made in many sizes, but the largest could carry up to twelve people and four tons (3629 kg) of cargo. People around the world now enjoy canoeing for fun. Modern canoes are made of **fiberglass** rather than natural materials, but they are built using the designs developed by Native people hundreds of years ago.

Canoes allowed European traders and explorers to travel farther into North America than their larger wooden boats allowed them to go. Canoes could travel through shallow waters and could be portaged across land.

Making trails

Each Native nation had a territory. Native people knew the safest and easiest ways to travel through their territories. Over time, they wore paths through forests and open areas, creating trails that marked the routes of animals and the best places to cross rivers and mountains. These trails also marked the quickest portage routes between lakes, rivers, and streams. By the time European immigrants arrived, there was a network of trails across North America. Immigrants followed these trails while looking for places to settle. For example, they followed many of the paths west during the 1700s and 1800s. Later, Native trails provided the routes that planners used to lay out railways, as well as paved roads and highways.

Many Native groups used snowshoes and toboggans to make traveling across snow easier.

Hunting and fishing

Native people hunted animals, which provided them with meat and fat for food, bones for making tools and weapons, and **hides**, or skins, for making clothing, blankets, and shelters. Native hunters spent their lives learning about the animals they hunted. They knew where to find the animals, which sounds the animals made, and how the animals behaved. The hunters used their knowledge to create effective hunting methods and tools, and they developed great skills in tracking and catching animals. Still, Native hunters usually killed only the animals they needed, and Native people used every part of each animal.

Making animal calls
Many animals make sounds to call to one another. Native hunters recognized these sounds and mimicked them to make animals curious and draw them out of hiding. Hunters practiced making animal calls until their voices sounded exactly like the voices of the animals. Hunters also made whistles and callers out of bone, clay, birch bark, or wood. These whistles and callers helped hunters mimic animal sounds. The hunters above are using duck callers to lure ducks toward them. Today, hunters still use callers to lure animals.

The European way

The early European settlers had different views about animals and hunting than did Native North Americans. In Europe, only the wealthiest people hunted, and they did it as a sport. Most of the colonists were not wealthy, so they had never hunted before. At first, they misunderstood why Native people spent so much time hunting. Many believed that hunting was a pastime rather than work. In time, however, the colonists realized that they needed to hunt in order to survive in their new home, and they adopted many Native hunting techniques. People still use many of these hunting techniques today.

*Some Native hunters used **camouflage** while hunting. They disguised their bodies with animal hides or antlers or tied plants to their bodies to blend in with their surroundings.*

Fishing lures
Native fishers crafted fishing lures out of shells, bones, or wood. The lures resembled small fish that were eaten by larger fish. The lures attracted the fish, which the fishers then caught. Fishers from some nations discovered that fish are attracted to food by smell, as well as by sight. They boiled herbs and rubbed them on their lures. These fishers invented the first scented lures, which people still use today.

Sports and games

Sports and games were important parts of life for the people of most nations. Native people valued team spirit, and they believed that play was good for both adults and children. These ideas continue to shape people's views of sports and games.

Lacrosse

The most famous Native sport is lacrosse. Lacrosse was played in many parts of North America, but no one is sure exactly which nation invented it. Lacrosse was not just played for fun. People from neighboring nations often played it as a way of settling disputes. Many nations also viewed playing lacrosse as a spiritual celebration. The first Europeans to see lacrosse were French **missionaries** in present-day Quebec. They gave the sport its name and eventually began playing it. Today, lacrosse is played in many countries around the world. It is Canada's national sport and is one of the fastest-growing sports in the United States.

Hockey

Some historians believe that the game of hockey was first played by Native people. The Native version of the game is known as **shinny**. People played shinny on fields or on ice with a wooden or a hide ball. They hit the ball using curved sticks or kicked it with their feet. French priests named the game "hockey." They thought the curved stick looked like a shepherd's hook-shaped staff or "hoquet."

The painting above shows Native people participating in sports and games. How many toys and games do you recognize? Some people are playing marbles. Native people played marble games using shells, dried berries, or small stones. Did you notice the toboggan-riders? People from many nations had fun in winter by sliding down snow-covered hills on toboggans.

Wah-pah-nah-yah
(Dick West)

Games and toys

Native children played many games that were similar to those played by European children, including hide-and-seek, string games, and cup-and-pin games. Native girls had dolls made of corn husks and other natural materials, whereas boys played with small bows and arrows. Native people also made several toys that colonists had never before seen, including toboggans, and spinning tops or "whirligigs." Colonists adopted these toys for their own children. The toys remained popular for hundreds of years.

Clothing and jewelry

Native people developed their own styles of clothing, footwear, and jewelry. Traditionally, people made these items from the natural materials around them, including animal hides, furs, shells, bones, and animal teeth. Over the years, Native clothing makers began using European materials, as well. Today, people across North America and in many other countries wear clothing that was invented by Native North Americans.

Fur traders and explorers adopted the fringed shirts and leggings many Native people wore. The clothing was made of animal hides. Fringe looked attractive, and many settlers found that it also helped draw rain off their clothing. Although tastes in fashion changed, fringed jackets and skirts continue to be popular.

Parkas

Inuit people, who live in the far North, invented warm, hooded jackets known as **parkas**. Traditional parkas were made of furry animal hides. Parkas were sometimes lined with bird skins that had the feathers still attached, to help trap people's body heat. Many modern parkas are made of nylon fabrics that are stuffed with duck or goose feathers.

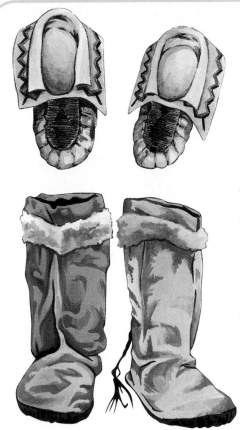

Moccasins

People of various nations designed a type of shoe that is known as a **moccasin**. Each nation had its own unique style of moccasin, but most were made from a single piece of animal hide that was cut to curl up around the foot. Moccasins were stitched around the top. This design helped keep feet warm and dry, since there were no seams around the bottom through which water could leak. Moccasins are famous for being comfortable and durable. Many people around the world still wear moccasins.

Mukluks

Mukluks are similar to moccasins, but they are tall boots rather than low shoes. These boots were invented by the Inuit and Yup'ik peoples. People still wear traditional mukluks, both for warmth and for fashion. Many people also wear winter boots that are designed to look like mukluks, but these boots are made of other materials such as plastic and nylon.

Silver and turquoise

People around the world value jewelry made of silver and **turquoise**. This intricate jewelry was first designed by Dineh (Navajo) silversmiths in the late 1870s. Soon after, Zuni and Hopi silversmiths began making silver-and-turquoise designs of their own. Artists of all three nations continue to make jewelry using new and traditional designs. Many people collect these pieces, which are considered to be both fashion and art.

Medicine and health

Native healers used herbs, fruits, leaves, roots, flowers, and bark to make medicines that relieved pain, helped heal wounds, or helped people recover from fevers, stomach problems, and other illnesses. Certain medicines also helped ease the minds of people who were anxious, upset, or grieving.

Traditionally, Native people have thought of well-being as the combination of a healthy body, mind, and spirit. They believe that illnesses are not always the result of problems within the body. For example, Native people believe that stress and other emotions can make people sick or stop them from recovering. Traditional Native remedies for diseases and other ailments are combinations of natural medicines and spiritual treatments. Many ideas about health and wellness today are similar to those held by Native people. These ideas are known as **holistic medicine**. Holistic medicine focuses on healing the whole person, instead of just the sickness or disease.

Bathing and hygiene

Native people had different ideas about bathing than did the European colonists. People of most Native nations bathed frequently, often every day. They believed that cleanliness of the body maintained good health. They also believed that bathing was a way of **purifying** themselves spiritually. Native people used soaps, shampoos, and hair conditioners made from ingredients that came from plants and animals. They cleaned their teeth by chewing the **resin** from trees and plants such as the ragged cup. They also rubbed their teeth with white clay or scrubbed them with frayed twigs. The early Europeans believed that bathing was unhealthy. Most bathed once or twice a year, if at all, and they rarely cleaned their teeth.

Jojoba, a plant Native people have used for centuries to soften skin and hair, is still a common ingredient in shampoos, conditioners, and skin creams.

Natural medicines

Colonists learned that Native people knew a lot about the plants and other natural materials in their territories. Many colonists were cured of illnesses by Native medicines, and these remedies became well-known **folk medicines** throughout the colonies. Native people used plants such as witch hazel, ginseng, cranberry, goldenseal, and saw palmetto as medicines. Today, more than 170 medicines are made from plants that were used by Native people.

Gifts of language

When Europeans arrived in North America, they saw many unfamiliar animals, plants, and landscapes. Often, they did not have names for the things they saw.

European explorers and immigrants created English words that were based on words from Native languages. They used these words to name places and objects that they had never before seen.

The name Canada is from a Haudenosaunee word "kanata," which means village. Six provinces and 26 states have native names.

Naming places

Colonists on the east coast of North America named places after their kings and queens, war heroes, saints, and other people they considered important. When Europeans later moved west, they often relied on Native guides. They learned from the guides that places already had names, and the European people also began to use these names. Places with Native names include Toronto (gathering place), Oregon (beautiful water), and Ohio (good river). Europeans also adopted Native names for many rivers, lakes, and mountains. They sometimes named areas, such as Kansas, Massachusetts, Illinois, and Utah, after nations who lived in these areas.

Words from Native languages

The list below contains some English words that came from Native languages:

bayou	husky	moccasin	pecan	skunk
caribou	mahogany	moose	peewee	squash
chinook	maize	mukluk	puma	succotash
chipmunk	manatee	okay	raccoon	tipi
hickory	mangrove	opossum	saguaro	wigwam
hominy	mesquite	parka	savanna	woodchuck

Code talkers

Some Native Americans used their languages to help the United States and its allies win World Wars I and II. These Native people served as **code talkers** in the Army and Navy. Code talkers were soldiers who sent and received coded messages by radio and then translated the messages. The messages contained information about troop locations, bombings, and where to aim attacks. In World War I, Choctaw soldiers sent and received these messages in their language. German soldiers listening in were never able to crack the "code" of the Choctaw language, unlike other codes used by the United States.

In World War II, Native Americans from the Choctaw, Dineh (Navajo), Comanche, Dakota, Lakota, and Nakota nations served as code talkers. Using words from their language, Dineh code talkers created a code that was used in battles throughout the Pacific region. Their code was so effective, that Japanese code breakers never cracked a single message! By helping keep plans and movements secret, the code talkers helped the United States win many battles that they could not have won otherwise. The United States government officially honored the Dineh code talkers in 1992. The story of the code talkers inspired a Hollywood movie called *Windtalkers*.

Land of the free

Long before colonists reached North America, Native nations had organized governments. Many Native nations had ideas about government, leadership, and freedom that surprised the colonists. Unlike European countries at the time, which were ruled by kings and queens, most Native nations were **democratic**, or had leaders that were chosen by the people. Leaders worked for the people and could be replaced if the people lost confidence in the abilities of the leaders. Unlike kings and queens, Native leaders could not force people to do things. They led only as long as people chose to follow them. The leaders of some nations joined together to form **confederacies**. A confederacy is a group of nations that work together to solve common problems, achieve common goals, and protect one another from enemies.

The Haudenosaunee Confederacy

One confederacy formed by Native nations was the Haudenosaunee Confederacy. It is also known as the Iroquois League, the Iroquois Confederacy, and the Six Nations. The Haudenosaunee Confederacy was made up originally of the Mohawk, Oneida, Onondaga, Cayuga, and Seneca nations. The Tuscarora nation joined in the early 1700s. Before the nations in the confederacy joined together, they were constantly at war. They agreed to form a confederacy to bring peace, justice, and equality to their people. Each nation in the confederacy ruled its own territory but agreed to share power and make decisions together. For example, all the nations had to agree when making decisions regarding war, trade agreements, new alliances, and other matters that involved all the nations in the confederacy.

The symbol of the Haudenosaunee Confederacy is the Tree of Peace guarded by an eagle. In its talons, the eagle holds five arrows—one for each of the first five nations to unite. There is a war club buried under the tree, which symbolizes "burying," or ending, war between the nations.

People of the Haudenosaunee nations continue to follow the Great Law of Peace today. It may be the oldest constitution in the world.

The Great Law of Peace

The nations in the Haudenosaunee Confederacy followed a **constitution** called the Great Law of Peace. The constitution was an agreement, which outlined many details of government, including how decisions were made, how leaders were chosen, and how new nations could be added to the confederacy. According to the Great Law, the women of each nation chose the men who served their nation by representing them at **councils**, or meetings. People could replace their representatives if they were not doing a good job. At councils, all the representatives had to agree before a decision could be made. This agreement helped prevent one nation from forcing the others into actions they did not support.

Native influences on colonial leaders

In 1776, thirteen colonies joined together and became a country—the United States of America. Colonial leaders needed a way to unite the colonies. Benjamin Franklin, Thomas Jefferson, and other leaders had studied the Haudenosaunee Confederacy, as well as European governments. They respected the way the Haudenosaunee nations governed themselves. When the colonial leaders established a new government and wrote the Declaration of Independence and the U.S. Constitution, they adopted several ideas from the Haudenosaunee Confederacy and its Great Law of Peace. These ideas include the **federal** system of government, putting limits on the government's power over people's daily lives, and the belief that people have rights and are all equal.

The eagle became a symbol of the United States government. The eagle holds thirteen arrows in its talons—one for each of the colonies that became the first states.

Native inspiration

In the past two hundred years, some important Americans and Canadians have been inspired by the examples set by Native people and their **societies**. Native societies have influenced women's rights, the League of Nations, and the Boy Scouts and Girl Guides.

The status of women

In most Native nations, women were respected and were considered equally important to men. Haudenosaunee women chose leaders and decided when leaders should be removed from power. They also ran their households and controlled their families' lands. Colonists had different ideas about women. They believed men were superior to women. Colonial men controlled the government and their homes. For more than a century, women in the United States were not allowed to vote or to own property.

Matilda Joslyn Gage wrote articles and gave speeches arguing that the roles of Haudenosaunee women proved that women are equal to men.

Inspiring the suffragettes

By the mid 1800s, women in the United States began demanding **suffrage**, or the right to vote. Some of the earliest **suffragettes**, including Matilda Joslyn Gage, Lucretia Mott, and Elizabeth Cady Stanton, lived in New York State near the Haudenosaunee nations. They learned about Haudenosaunee societies and admired the role and influence of women in them. Inspired by the examples set by wise and powerful Haudenosaunee women, the suffragettes held their first meeting in Seneca Falls, New York, in 1848. After struggling for many years, American women finally won the right to vote in federal elections in 1920.

International cooperation

After World War I ended in 1918, many countries, including Great Britain and France wanted to form an organization that encouraged countries to work together and settle disagreements peacefully. The countries formed the League of Nations. The league was set up using ideas from the United States Constitution, which had, in turn, taken ideas from the Haudenosaunee Confederacy. The League of Nations was the early version of the **United Nations**, which was formed in 1945 after the end of World War II.

The Boy Scouts and Girl Guides

In 1902, Ernest Thompson Seton began a boys' club, called the Woodcraft League of America, to teach boys the value of honesty, strength, and independence—traits he saw in Native men. Boys in the League practiced many skills adopted from Native nations, including building shelters, using bows and arrows, canoeing, and tracking animals. When they succeeded, boys received feathers and badges to wear on a sash.

The idea for the badges came from the **Plains nations**, who used similar rewards for their young men. Seton tried to spread the Woodcraft League to England, but a group called the British Boy Scout Association was already popular there. The Boy Scouts club came to the United States in 1908. The Woodcraft League became part of it, and the Boy Scouts adopted many of the ideas and values of the League. The Girl Guides formed in 1910, using many of the same ideas and values.

Respecting the Earth

Although each Native nation had its own traditions and values, all of the nations shared similar views of nature. Native people have always believed that all things in nature—people, plants, animals, rocks, water, and the land—are connected. Most non-Native western societies have begun to see the value of this belief only within the past 50 years.

The land is not ours

Native people of various nations share the belief that the Earth belongs to future generations. They believe that each person must protect the land and make sure there are plants, animals, and other resources for people in the future. This belief was and is an important part of Native people's spirituality, and it has shaped their daily lives.

European ideas

Before Europeans arrived, Native people usually took only what they needed from nature. This idea is now known as **conservation**. Europeans arriving in North America had different views about nature. They thought nature was something people had to **conquer**, or defeat. They believed that trees, plants, animals, and other parts of nature were put on Earth to be used by people. Most Europeans were amazed by the vast numbers of trees and animals in North America. They thought they could take all they wanted without ever running out.

Changing ideas

In the past 60 years, non-Native societies have begun to see that human beings are part of nature and not separate from it. In the 1950s, a new science, called **ecology**, developed from this belief. Ecology is the study of the relationship between living things and their environments.

Traditions proven true

Ecologists have proven what Native people have always believed: when something happens to one part of nature, it changes the rest of nature. For example, ecologists realized that destroying forests, polluting air and water, and causing animals and plants to become **extinct** affects all life on Earth, including the lives of people. Today, more and more people are becoming interested in traditional Native ideas about the Earth and our place on this planet.

Native people believed that the resources they used were gifts from nature. They were thankful for these gifts and were careful not to take too much from the natural world.

Lasting wisdom

People all over the world appreciate Native art. This contemporary painting by Lois Beardslee is titled "Manabouzhou Creating the Fishes."

Lessons, ideas, tools, and knowledge can be gifts only if people are willing to accept them. Although the world has already received many gifts from Native North Americans, there are many more that may be appreciated. Traditional Native beliefs and practices can offer people of various backgrounds different ways of seeing the world and thinking about it. For example, people are now studying traditional Native farming methods in order to reduce the use of **pesticides** and other chemicals, which are harmful to the environment.

Continuing to contribute

Native people across the United States and Canada continue to make important contributions to the world. Some share their nation's traditional knowledge and beliefs, from which everyone can learn lessons. Some craft art or jewelry, that not only brings beauty to the world, but also shares important ideas. Other Native people teach others about the many things Native people have accomplished and are continuing to accomplish.

A new appreciation for old gifts

In the past, most non-Native people did not appreciate Native art and music because they believed European culture was better. Fortunately, Native people have kept their traditional arts, instruments, dances, and songs alive. Today, many people appreciate the beauty of these gifts.

Buffy Sainte-Marie is a successful singer and artist and is also an advocate for Native rights and education.

Wilma Mankiller created the Institute for Cherokee Literacy. The Institute has helped the Cherokee people preserve their language and traditions.

Today many Native people participate in ceremonies that were celebrated by their ancestors. Dancing is part of these ceremonies.

Glossary

Note: Boldfaced words that are defined in the book may not appear in the glossary.

adopting Taking an idea or an object and using it as one's own

alliance An association of two or more groups of people formed to benefit one another

biodegradable Describing something that can break down naturally and become part of the Earth

camouflage Colors or markings that help something blend in with its surroundings

colonist A person who lives in a colony

economy A country's money and resources

elder An older, respected member of a family, group, or nation

extinct Describing a plant or animal species that no long exists on Earth

federal A form of government in which states join together and give power to a central unit while retaining certain powers for themselves

fiberglass A strong material made of thin threads of glass

folk medicine Traditional medicines, including natural and herbal medicines

fur trade A system of trade in which items were exchanged for animal furs

missionary A priest or other religious person who travels from place to place to convert people to a religion

pesticides Harmful chemicals that kill insects

Plains nations The Native nations, such as the Sioux, that lived on the Great Plains

prejudice Unfair or untrue ideas and opinions

purify To make pure or clean

resin A sticky substance, which does not dissolve in water, that oozes out of some plants

society A group of people who share a culture

suffragette A woman seeking the right to vote through organized protest

technology Methods and devices that are used for practical purposes

territory An area of land and water on which a group of people traditionally lived, hunted, fished, and gathered foods

translator A person who explains the meaning of words in a language to people who do not speak that language

turquoise A mineral that is blue-green in color, which can be used to make jewelry

United Nations An international organization of countries founded in 1945 that promotes world peace, security, and cooperation

Index

1 2 3 4 5 6 7 8 9 0   Printed in the U.S.A.   4 3 2 1 0 9 8 7 6 5